IEP JĀLTOK

Volume 80

Sun Tracks

An American Indian Literary Series

Series Editor

Ofelia Zepeda

IEP JĀLTOK

POEMS FROM A MARSHALLESE DAUGHTER

≋

KATHY JETÑIL-KIJINER

THE UNIVERSITY OF
ARIZONA PRESS

TUCSON

A special thanks to Wilbert Alik for his help editing the Marshallese text.

The University of Arizona Press
www.uapress.arizona.edu

Printed in the United States of America

ISBN-13: 978-0-8165-3402-9 (paper)

Cover design by Leigh McDonald
Cover photo of weaver Betty Lobwij by Milañ Loeak.

Publication of this book is made possible in part by the proceeds of a permanent
endowment created with the assistance of a Challenge Grant from the National
Endowment for the Humanities, a federal agency.

Library of Congress Cataloging-in-Publication Data
Names: Jetñil-Kijiner, Kathy, author.
Title: Iep jāltok : poems from a Marshallese daughter / Kathy Jetñil-Kijiner.
Other titles: Poems from a Marshallese daughter | Sun tracks ; v. 80.
Description: Tucson : The University of Arizona Press, 2017. | Series: Sun tracks : An
    American Indian literary series ; volume 80. | Some text in Marshallese.
Identifiers: LCCN 2016031577 | ISBN 9780816534029 (pbk. : alk. paper)
Subjects: LCSH: Marshall Islands—Poetry. | Protest poetry. | LCGFT: Poetry.
Classification: LCC PR9670.M373 J474 2017 | DDC 821/.92—dc23
LC record available at https://lccn.loc.gov/2016031577

♾ This paper meets the requirements of ANSI/NISO Z39.48-1992 (Permanence of
Paper).

*This book is dedicated to my mother,
my first and most infinite source of inspiration.*

CONTENTS

IEP JĀLTOK

Basket   4
Lōktañūr   6
Liwātuonmour   8
Lidepdepju   9
Ettoḷọk Ilikin Lọmeto   10

HISTORY PROJECT

Hooked   14
The letter B is for   19
History Project   20
Fishbone Hair   24

LESSONS FROM HAWAI'I

Flying to Makiki Street   34
My Rosy Cousin   36
To Laura Ingalls Wilder   37
Bursts of Bianca   39
On the Couch with Būbū Neien   42
Lessons from Hawai'i   45
The Monkey Gate   50
Lost at Sea   53
Crash   54
Last Days in the Bay   56

TELL THEM

Spoken Marshallese Lesson Nine   58
Just a Rock   59
Campaigning in Aur   60
Tell Them   64
Lavender Saltwater   68
Dear Matafele Peinam   70
There's a Journalist Here   74
Two Degrees   76
Basket   80

IEP JĀLTOK

Iep jāltok (yiyip jalteq).
"A basket whose opening is facing the speaker."
Said of female children. She represents a basket whose
contents are made available to her relatives. Also refers
to matrilineal society of the Marshallese.

—MARSHALLESE ENGLISH DICTIONARY

*My mother once told me girls represent wealth
for their families.*

"Girls continue the lineage."

BASKET

woman tip your lid
across the table
you swell
with offering

you

offer

offer

offer

earth
of your
mother

roots
of your
father

you

thin
dried
strips of
leaves

the next
basket

waiting
to be
woven

woman tip your lid
towards the table
you swell
with offering
            you
                    offer
                        offer
                            offer

                                    scrape
                                    your floor
                                    bare

                                        vessel?

                                            receptacle
                                            littered
                                            with scraps
                                            tossed by
                                            others

                                    i fell asleep
                                    dreamt

                            my smile
                        was merely
                    a rim
                woven
            into my
    face

LŌKTAÑŪR

I.

The sail
that powers
the Marshallese canoe

feeds our family
fights our wars
claims our land
visits clans

came from

a Mother

II.

1. And so it was that the Irooj's wife Lōktañūr gave birth to ten sons who all lived on the island of Wōja. **2.** One day the sons argued, voices clapping like thunder against the trees. **3.** And they said Who will be Irooj of this Island? **4.** And the eldest, Tūṃur, said Why don't we have a canoe race to the island of Je? The first to reach the island will be Irooj, he said. **5.** As the brothers lined up on the beach, carved canoes pointed towards a sea swallowing the sun their Mother Lōktañūr walked up to them. **6.** And Lōktañūr struggling with a bundle in her arms asked My Son will you take me with you? **7.** And Tūṃur looked at the bundle and said Ask my younger brother. **8.** And the younger brother said Ask my younger brother who said the same thing. **9.** She will only slow me down. **10.** And so on. **11.** Ask Jebrọ! The brothers laughed. He is the youngest! He will lose anyway! **12.** And Jebrọ, with his back to the swirling sea said Yes Mother I will take you with me. **13.** As the brothers paddled furious against the salt biting at the wood of their paddles Lōktañūr, standing on the canoe with her son Jebrọ, began to unravel the bundle slowly the way the sun unravels its silky rays. **14.** And Jebrọ said What is that Mother? **15.** And Lōktañūr said Behold my Son. **16.** This is what shall be called the Sail.

LIWĀTUONMOUR

1. And so it was that Liwātuonmour and Lidepdepju were sisters who were birthed by fire and sea. **2.** They came, long, long ago. **3.** From the land of Ep they came, weathered rough by hands of salt. **4.** They came, glaring from the westward sun. **5.** Liwātuonmour and Lidepdepju, mothers of the chiefly lineage, mothers of the Irooj. **6.** Mothers who shaped the sounds of midday and dusk. **7.** They found the words inside their blood inside their pulse inside the stars and the waves. **8.** Some say they were goddesses. **9.** But one missionary said they were nothing more. Than rocks. Nothing more. Than stone. **10.** Dr. Rife threw Liwātuonmour's stone body into the ocean. **11.** She felt herself engulfed. By the ocean. Swallowed. **12.** She drifted further and further. Below the waves. Down to where. The silence. Echoes. **13.** And she watched the bottom of Dr. Rife's canoe turn. And sail away. **14.** And she herself turned. And welcomed the earth. That churned and birthed her. **15.** You see the missionary said as he came to shore. **16.** Nothing more. Than a rock. **17.** Lidepdepju was now alone. **18.** Lidepdepju was alone. In rage. **19.** And the people chanted. **20.** And the chant pulsed through the island. **21.** Luerkolik ej no diuñ ña duireañ. Lidepdepju erbet inij eo. **22.** The reef is destroying me because of our sin to Lidepdepju. She is destroying us all. Lidepdepju is destroying our fleet of canoes.

LIDEPDEPJU

Let me take you out to see Lidepdepju
through overgrown leaves winding
breadfruit trees and twisting pandanus
slapping at mosquitoes and red ants that sting
sand and dirt itching your toes,
through that clearing, follow
the roar of the ocean

there

is Lidepdepju, standing
alone deep
in water
firm
in ocean floor
between our shore
and the next

This is our gift for you, Lidepdepju—
baskets of fresh bwiro, salted fish
The finest jaki caress
basalt calluses of your skin
We are here
to pay tribute, to ask
for your guidance
We are here
to ask for your strength

Lidepdepju we are here

to sharpen
              our spears
                          for war

ETTOḶOK ILIKIN ḶOMETO

Below are the lyrics to one of the many songs written by my great-grandfather, Carl Heine, called "Juon Wot Eṃṃan." He wrote it while he was living in the Marshall Islands as a missionary. We continue to sing this song today during family gatherings. In the left column are the original lyrics in Marshallese; in the right column are the lyrics translated to English by my mother.

Ettoḷok ilikin ḷometo	Far away over the ocean
Eo ḷok wōt,	Even farther,
Ej pād aelōñ eo eṃṃan tata	Is the homeland that is best
Ijo iaar ḷotak ie	Where I was born
Ij keememej ijo iaar bed ie	I remember where I was
Ke iaar ajiri	When I was a child
Iṃweo iturin kiap ko rōnaaj	The house by the fragrant lilies
Ijo iaar ḷotak ie	The house where I was born
Aelōñ otemjej rōnana,	Another home is not as good
Juon wōt eṃṃan	Only one is the best
Jera men eḷap aō oñ kake	My friends that I miss
Bwe in lo aelōñ eo ao	I can see them in my homeland
Ke ij ito-itak ioon laḷ in	As I roam the world
Ij būroṃōj	I am sad
In jepḷaak ñan ippan ro jatū	And want to return to my younger siblings
Im oñ kōn ro nukū	And yearn for my family
Ñāāt inaaj roñ ainikien jinō	When will I hear my mother's voice
Kūr tok ñan eō,	Calling to me
Ñāāt inaaj bar kweḷok im nukū	When will I see again my family
Ilo ṃweo iṃō	In my own home?

Ettoḷọk ilikin ḷọmeto Jiṃṃa Carl was a marine garden *Eo ḷọk wot, ej pād aelōñ eo eṃṃan tata* A culture of aqua hands pruning giant clams barnacled mouths wide open unblinking eye of the reef watching always watching *Ijo iaar ḷotak ie* Once german once australian once a rash and bold current flowing in from the east *Ij keememej ijo iaar pād ie* Now father of a harsh tongue a soggy Bible *Ke iaar ajiri* Father of a used canoe *Iṃweo iturin kiap ko rōnaaj* She must have been beautiful *Ijo iaar ḷotak ie* Bubu Arbella was tall straight hair to knees an unclear face a vacant voice *Aelōñ otemjej rōnana* What else was she where are her wild letters sprouting from sand *Juon wōt eṃṃan* After pushing and pushing and pushing she snapped in two torn open she sprouted wings and Jiṃṃa could not find her *Jera men eḷap aō oñ kake* He lost her Jiṃṃa lost his wife *Bwe in lo aelin eo ao* He wandered for a year searching *Kei ij ito-itak ioon laḷ in* He found Būbū Neñij *Ij būroṃōj* Būbū Neñij was not as beautiful as her sister *In jepḷaak ñan ippān ro jatū* Short thick kinky hair an unclear face a vacant voice *Im oñ kōn ro nukū* Was she ever afraid that she was just a shadow *Ñāāt inaaj roñ ainikien jinō* Of what he lost before *Kor tok no io* Jiṃṃa was a used canoe he heard the call of other atolls searching for God *Ñāāt inaaj roñ ainikien jinō* Būbū was a barnacled mouth a pair of unblinking reef eyes waiting *Ilo ṃweo iṃo* Always waiting

HISTORY PROJECT

HOOKED

I.

After he felt the rain of bombs
that left puddles of silver shrapnel, slivers of
splinters where houses once stood and charred
bodies—both Japanese and Marshallese—

after he watched soldiers shoot
a woman's ears off
because her husband
was a deserter, an accused traitor,

after he watched his chief, strung up
by his ankles, beaten raw for stealing
from a dwindling supply of coconuts,

after fugitive nights, when fishing was banned,
when he'd slip onto the reef flat, breathless,
the moon curved, shining like
the outlawed fishhook, gripped tight
between his fingers

and after nights when even this
became dangerous, after the children
stopped asking for his stolen catch of fish,
after even they had withered away,
rows of ribs smiling
grotesque grins through skin

after all of that
it must have seemed
heaven sent
a gift from God
this gift from the Americans,
this shining tower

of food
placed before him
box after box after box
of canned spam, flaky biscuits
chocolate bars, dry sausages, hard candy and
bags and bags of rice all waiting
to be eaten

he remembers
he cried
it was so
beautiful

II.

Every day of the life he led after he remembers
that pile of food taller
than any building he had ever seen

he remembers it as he slices spam, sizzling
hot on the pan, he remembers it
as he drizzles soy sauce
into a boiling pot of crispy ramen

he remembers it as he pops
open a can of vienna sausage, savors
the salty grease on his warm rice, the taste
of a filled belly

III.

And even after
his breathing
turned heavy
even after his joints
protested the walk to the store
even after the devious tingle trickled
into his arms, even after
the doctors
told him the leg

would have to go,
even then

he never
stopped
licking the grease
from his fingers
that still felt haunted
by the outlawed

hook.

IV.

When his children asked him why
he wouldn't, couldn't listen, why
he kept eating the food his doctors
had prescribed against, even after
they begged,

he merely
flexed
his restless
fingers.

He had been hungry.
He would never be hungry again.

THE LETTER B IS FOR

baaŋ (baham). From Engl. 2(inf, tr
-e) 3,4,6*(-i)*. Bomb. As in

Kobaaŋ ke?

        Are you contaminated

                with radioactive fallout?

HISTORY PROJECT

At fifteen I decide
to do my history project
on nuclear testing in the Marshall Islands
time to learn my own history

I weave through book after article after website
all on how the U.S. military once used
my island home
for nuclear testing
I sift through political jargon
tables of nuclear weapons
with names like Operation Bravo
Crossroads
and Ivy
quotes from american leaders like
> *90,000 people are out there. Who*
> *gives a damn?*

I'm not mad
I already knew all of this

I glance at a photograph
of a boy, peeled skin
arms legs suspended
a puppet
next to a lab coat lost
in his clipboard

I read firsthand accounts
of what we call
jelly babies
tiny beings with no bones
skin—red as tomatoes
the miscarriages gone unspoken
the broken translations
> *I never told my husband*
> *I thought it was my fault*

I thought
there must be something
wrong
inside me

I flip through snapshots
of american marines and nurses branded
white with bloated grins sucking
beers and tossing beach balls along
our shores
and my islander ancestors, cross-legged
before a general listening
to his fairy tale
about how it's
          for the good of mankind
to hand over our islands
let them blast
radioactive energy
into our sleepy coconut trees
our sagging breadfruit trees
our busy fishes that sparkle like new sun
into our coral reefs
brilliant as an aurora borealis woven
beneath a glassy sea

          God will thank you they told us

yea
as if God Himself
ordained
those powdered flakes
to drift
onto our skin hair eyes
to seep into our bones

We mistook radioactive fallout
for snow

          God will thank you they told us

like God's just been

waiting
for my people
to vomit
all of humanity's sins
onto impeccable white shores
gleaming
like the cross burned
into our open
scarred palms

at one point in my research
I stumble on a photograph
of goats
tied to american ships
bored and munching on tubs of grass

At the bottom a caption read

> *Goats and pigs were left on naval ships as test subjects.*
> *Thousands*
> *of letters flew in from america*
> *protesting*
>
> *animal abuse.*

At 15
I want radioactive energy megatons of tnt and a fancy degree
anything and everything I could ever need
to send ripples of death through a people who put goats
before human beings
so their skin
can shrivel
beneath the glare
of hospital room lights
three generations later
as they watch their grandfather/aunty/cousin's life drip
across that same
black
screen
knots
of knuckles

tied
to steel beds
cold
and absent
of any breath

But I'm only
15

so I finish my project
graph my people's death by cancer
on flow charts
in 3-D
gluestick my ancestors' voice
onto a posterboard I bought from office max
staple tables screaming
the 23 millions of dollars stuffed
into our mouths
generation
        after generation
                after generation
and at the top
I spray painted in bold stenciled yellow
FOR THE GOOD OF MANKIND

and entered it in the school district-wide competition called
History Day

my parents were quietly proud
and so was my teacher
and when the three balding white judges
finally
came around to my project
one of them looked at it and said
        Yea . . .
        but it wasn't really
        for the good of mankind, though
        was it?

and I lost.

FISHBONE HAIR

I.

Inside my niece Bianca's old room I found

two ziplocks
stuffed
with rolls and rolls of hair

dead as a doornail black as a tunnel hair thin
as strands of tumbling seaweed

Maybe it was my sister
who stashed away Bianca's locks in ziplock bags
locked it away so no one could see
trying to save that
rootless hair
that hair without a home

II.

There had been a war
raging inside Bianca's six year old bones
white cells had staked their flag
they conquered the territory of her tiny body
they saw it as their destiny
they said it was manifested

                                    It

                        all

                                 fell

                                        out

III.

I felt

bald

and blank

as Bianca's

skull

when they closed

her casket

hymns

wafting

into the night sky

IV.

Bianca loved
to eat fish
she ate it raw ate it fried ate it whole
she ate it with its head
slurping on the eyeball jelly
leaving only
tiny
neat
bones

V.

The marrow

should have worked

They said she had

six months

to live

VI.

That's what the doctors told the fishermen
over 50 years ago
when they were out at sea
just miles
away from Bikini
the day the sun
exploded
split open
and rained ash
on the fishermen's clothes

On that day those fishermen
were quiet
they were neat
they dusted the ash
out of their hair
reeled in their fish

and turned around their motorboat to speed home

VII.

There is an old Chamorro legend
that the women of Guåhan saved their island
from a giant coral eating fish
by hacking off their
long and black as the night sky hair

They wove their locks
into a massive magical net

They caught the monster fish

and they saved their islands

VIII.

Thin

            rootless

                     fishbone hair

      black

        night

                              sky

         catch

                     ash

                 catch

                      moon

            catch

      star

for you Bianca
for you

LESSONS FROM HAWAI'I

FLYING TO MAKIKI STREET

Night lights peer into your oval window
and you, cousin, are sobs buried
beneath the cover of an itchy airplane blanket.

Leavemealone!
stings
my palm from your shoulder.
It evaporates slow
into this arid cabin cradling us
across the Pacific
from the Marshall Islands to Hawai'i—
your new home.

My nine year old mind is desperate.
It wonders if sticks of juicy fruit gum
could chew away
the raw ache in your heart.

Or maybe while we peel open
the wrapper of some ametama, wrap
our teeth in sticky coconut rounds,
we could find some way
to peel apart the loss
of your old home,
your house by the reef.

Do you mourn that reef?
That leathered dark brown edge
of Rita? Do you mourn the sun
burning like coils on a rusted stove?
Do you miss Rita's tin roofs,
its unpainted walls and the children
who know the joy of rainstorms in heat?
Do you miss your father, placid
in his blank wooden chair, chanting
family histories until the night turns deep?

Cousin let's stretch those nights
to Makiki Street, with its pine trees
bunkbed whispers and jawaiian music blaring
beneath damp Hawaiian rainbows.
How we will fade into homework, classes,
schedules with tennis practice,
band practice, ROTC, college preparatory

and your McDonald's uniforms
folded
starched
every night—always so
neat.

How our lives
will be just like that:
folded
starched every
bare night—so nice and
neat.

It won't be so bad cousin.

Trust me.

MY ROSY COUSIN

My cousin is bloody roses tatted / on her ankle / her knuckles
white as rice / gripping the steering wheel / cruising
thru manoa / sunglasses ignoring those redred lights

My cousin is one cold pepsi one chocolate hershey bar /
the daily ransom for driving me to school / *let's make*
a quickstop / pitstop / 7-eleven / gimme your money /
you live with your parents / you don't gotta pay rent

My cousin is four a.m. taptaptaps on the window / slurred threats /
Kōppeḷọk e kōjām eṇ / kwōnaaj loe / passed out on the front lawn /
mom's pissed again / *rūtto pata* tossed between aunties lips /
when will she ever learn / coffee cups and morning gossip

My cousin is bullying / *dede you're so stupid / dede you're so useless /*
other times she cuts/ straight thru bone / *dede you're as white / white /*
white as they come / i mean what other marshallese writes /
poetry and plays piano

My cousin goes to college / talks about classes with hawaiian teachers
and tongan scholars / tells us tragic samoan love stories and funny
fijian satires / *doesn't that sound just like home / doesn't that sound*
just like majuro

My cousin asked me to write a poem / a poem about her / and i said that i would /
so this is a poem / about how i bloomed / inside her voice / inside her stories /
this is also about how i was pruned / cut raw / dripping bloody / just like her
ankle red roses

TO LAURA INGALLS WILDER

Don't know why
I chose the prairie
but in the third grade I was not
a Marshallese girl lonely
in the metropolis maze of Hawai'i
but a spunky white girl in Minnesota
roughing it through bleak homestead lands
and braving the sharp bite of swarming blizzards

I had never seen snow in my life
the only river
was the Makiki stream by our apartment complex
It smelled like frogs burping and bubbled
cool at our bare ankles and slippered feet
My cousins and I chased darting mongoose tails
stole juicy starfruit from neighbors
and when humidity dried our lips
we snuck into the pool in the next apartment over
frog-stroked through chlorine water

And still, I buried my tomboy yearnings
between the pages of a girl who seemed
like me—ran through grass in bare feet
skinned knees ripped dresses and
scoffed at wedding vows

But I remained confused
at Ma's consistent warning
Don't forget your bonnet Laura—
you don't want to turn brown
like an Indian!
I looked at the back of my own brown hand and
interrogated my mother
for bonnets and hoop skirts
demanded that my father play the fiddle
by an open fire, dismissed

his fresh cut sashimi and craved
what I imagined
to be the succulent meat of geese

Ten years later and a chapter
out of the fourth novel of the series
Little House in Town
still burns like a scar
reopened

A minstrel show starring
Pa and his friends!
The entire town cheering,
guffawing in glee
as their fathers smeared
black grease
on white faces
rolled blue eyes and
snorted across stage
drumming sticks and hollering
to the bleating wails of organ music
What a fun night!

What else
was tucked away between the pages
lost in rushes of calico skirts, corsets, and hay stacks?

Where exactly
were all the Indians, Laura
when you wagon wobbled cross country
to Kansas
the Indian territory?

Miles of prairie away
was the wheezing heave of hundreds
of displaced feet
little girls with tree bark hands
sun browned
              like me.

BURSTS OF BIANCA

for dad

When you come through the door, she
is a burst
of smiles sunny afternoons giggle glitter
and deepdeep eyes deepdeep dimples
that radiate
from her
starchy
crinkled gown

She is 10
Notice a feeding tube snakes
into her nose, an iv breaks
the skin of her wrist
Notice the twist of her fists in her sheets

But don't feel too much just listen
because she's trying to tell you a story
about the day she was sent to the principal's office
for yelling at a dumb boy
for copying her homework

The nurse breezes in and you
are startled but she
keeps going

She never complains
about the
chemotherapy she just
keeps going

This is not uncommon
You remind yourself
This situation?
Not so rare

Most Marshallese
can say they've mastered the language of cancer
Bianca doesn't know much English
and yet she knows
what blood cells mean
what bone marrow, catheter
and remission therapy means

You think about this as you stare at Bianca
Rainbows of bracelet beads budding
across her hospital blanket

But today you and Bianca will not
be discussing the effects of nuclear testing
Or colonization
Or the cancers that shadow your people

Instead you will discuss Spongebob
You will construct paper card castles
Craft the best pudding and ketchup stew
Kaleidoscope colors across her nails
Use her blanket for a sail

You won't talk about her aches
her untouched plate
the sunrays she can no longer seek
or that funeral
that chokes your dreams

and when visiting hours are over it's
not easy
it's harder than you'd think

The nuzzled kiss
The frumpled tight tight hug
The cross your heart pinky promise
You'll be back
Yes you promise
You promise and promise her

You will
be back

And as you leave
the door clicks shut behind you
and suddenly
it's harder to breathe

ON THE COUCH WITH BŪBŪ NEIEN

After six years of living in Hawai'i,
I return to Majuro to find myself
sitting on a couch
with my grandmother, my būbū Neien
sweating in jeans, my hands folded tight
while questions nag the bones of my skull.

Crouched coughing,
hacking, fidgeting
with her embroidered handkerchief, she
is a paper doll, crumpled
into a heap, shivering
in the heat.
Her dark bruised skin melts
away from her face.

My grandmother has tongue cancer.

Words
are ripped
from the belly
of her throat
before they can be born.
Before they can flutter
in this space
between us—
an unturned layer of earth I
can no longer cultivate.

I can't speak fluent Marshallese.
English syllables accent
the walls of my voice, pronounce me
Ashamed
so I bury my native tongue
beneath a borrowed one.

The silence roars
between us like
the steel fan spinning sunlight
across her red linoleum floor

and I wanna tell my grandmother that I wish
our voices didn't yearn for language,
that her stories could be netted
from the depth of her brown eyes,
a water that runs deeper
than the shallow
rattle of her breath.

I wish I could ask Būbū
if she remembers when pink
was my favorite color.
When my light-up sneakers squeaked
and ribbons on my tricycle streamed
pink. I wish I could ask

if there was pink
across the roof of the sun's mouth
yawning over her childhood home—
Aelōñḷapḷap, its reef a curved smile to the sky.

I wish I could ask about the ache
of fingers caked hard, crooked from days
of soap and iron washboards.
Būbū what was that like?

And when it turned to night did voices
scrape the tin roof of your dreams? The voices
with names fading like stars into darkness,
the warriors healers canoe carvers buried
before you?

So many questions
to be asked and answered, but
before my thoughts

can implode
Būbū Neien's hand
reaches over
pats
my knee.

She smiles,
lips stretched
across crinkles.

She hands me a small bundle
of embroidered handkerchiefs
just the like the one she uses.

She points
to the blossoming stitches
along the borders of the terry cloth and then
she giggles.
(She did them herself)

And suddenly sunlight
floods my insides
Thank you, Būbū,
I say. *Koṃṃool.*

And she folds
the softness of her palm
over mine, rests
her head against my shoulder
with a sigh.

Three months later, in the coolness
of my dim Hawai'i room, I imagine
the white floral print that must be dancing
along her arms. I imagine
the crinkle of the paper flowers and
the bent knees, the fold of her palms
on her still chest and the water
of her brown eyes closed, finally.

LESSONS FROM HAWAI'I

inspired by Emelihter Kihleng's poem "Micronesian Question"

LESSON NUMBER 1:

> *Fuckin Micronesians!*
that's my seventh grade friend
cussin at the boys across the street rockin
swap meet blue t-shirts
baggy jeans
spittin a steady beetlenut stream
> *You know,*
> *you're actually*
> *kinda smart*
> *for a Micronesian*
And that's my classmate
who I tutor through the civil war
through the first immigrants
through history that always
seems
to repeat itself

LESSON NUMBER 2:

Micronesian
MICRO
(nesian)
as in small.
tiny crumbs of islands scattered
across the Pacific Ocean.
Too many countries / cultures / nations no one
has heard about / cares about / too small
to notice.
Small like how
I feel
when the lady at the salon
delicately tracing white across my nail
stops and says

You don't look
Micronesian.
            You're much prettier!

LESSON NUMBER 3:

Prettier as in
not
ugly
like those
other
Micronesian girls
who are always
walking by the street
smiling rows
of gold teeth like they got
no shame
with hair greased and braided
cascading down dirt roads of brown skin
down shimmering dresses called guams
and neon colored Pohnpeian skirts
and I can hear
the disgust
in my cousin's voice
            Look at those girls!
            They wear their guams
            to school and to the store like they're
            at home
            Don't they
            know?
            This
            isn't their
            country.
            This
            is America.
            You see that
            is why everyone here
            hates
            us Micronesians!

LESSON NUMBER 4:

I'll tell you
why everyone here
hates
us Micronesians

It's cuz we're neon colored skirts screaming
Different

Different like that ESL kid
whose name you can't pronounce
whose accent you can't miss

Different like walmart / 7-eleven / mickey D's
parking lot kick its and fights
those long hours
those blue collar nights

Different like parties
with hundreds
of swarming aunties, uncles, cousins
sticky breadfruit drenched in creamy coconut
coolers of our favorite fish
wheeled from the airport
barbequed on a spit
my uncle waving me over

> *Dede a itok—*
> *kōjro ṃōñā!*
> *Dede come—*
> *let's eat!*

LESSON NUMBER 5:

Headline:
NO ALOHA FOR MICRONESIANS

MICRONESIANS RUN UP HEFTY HEALTH CARE TAB

MICRONESIANS FILL HOMELESS SHELTERS

We shoulda jus nuked their islands when we had the chance!

You know, they're better off living homeless in Hawai'i
than they are living in their own islands

Eh, eh—why did
the Micronesian man marry
a monkey?
Because all Micronesian women are monkeys!

What?

Can't you take a joke?

LESSON NUMBER 6:

It's actually
NOT Micronesian
It's Marshallese
Chuukese
Yapese
Pohnpeian
Palauan
Kosraean
Nauruan
Chamorro
Kiribati
but when Hawai'i insists
on lumping us
all together

when they belittle us and tell us we're small
when they tell us our people are small
when they give us a blank face
when they give us a closed door
when so many

in Hawai'i
hate
Micronesians
when so many
hate
us

LESSON NUMBER 7:

That's how I learned
That's how I learned
That's how I learned
to hate

me.

THE MONKEY GATE

I.

My uncle tells the story
of being lost in the Honolulu airport
how he fished out a wandering airport employee
and asked him if he knew where the Micronesian gate was
The man smirked through blue uniform
You mean the monkey gate?

Blood rushing beneath his
face blank and unchanged he turned
and jogged in the direction the man had pointed

II.

Alarms sound off
Three o'clock in the morning our bodies buzz
from cramped beds pull-out couches and flowery futons
we rise
shove swap meet t-shirts frozen steak
macadamia chocolates and extra cases
of our lives into solid trustworthy
coolers snapped shut and bound with
luminescent strands of tape
We pack
everything
into battered minivans and bucking SUVs
And as we sail along blank roads
we watch the landscape of apartment complexes
that loom above dozing bars, blinking 7-elevens and mini marts

Ķǫruji ledik ņe. Wake her up.

Our eyes flicker open to muttering cousins
The harsh lights of the Honolulu Airport
flood through the milky translucence of the window
as we drain our belongings from slide and shut doors
we chatter away nerves
rumbling and rolling in our bellies
At the check-in gate
Kosraean cousins argue over coolers that weigh too much
a Pohnpeian suit urgently checks his watch while
bony kneed brown children run   leap across
carts and piles of suitcases coolers boxes guarded
by graying Chuukese and Marshallese women
Whole families crouch and recline on the linoleum floor
We slide our slippers off

We make ourselves comfortable prop up ashy feet
The line to check in is long and
bag check even longer
Saying good-bye are one arm hugs and tears
sweating slow off our skin
And we are sad to see each other leave
And we are happy to see each other leave

We wave to the airport employees
We thank them
for handing us our tickets and carry-ons
and with upright backs
We smile
stroll
past security

LOST AT SEA

Sacramento
is palms slappin
thighs piit to piit beaten
men who beat your mother
beat to beat jus walk out walk it out
to jesus anthems babyblue lavalavas sarong
songs ambassadors of christianity praise the lord
spread the word of forced open thighs knocked up baby
blues how you get them fresh nikes how you get them bargain
bags of white rice white cans of tuna white envelopes pummeling
fists of numbers and bills tangled in bills for fatherless boys who head
households swallow that fear gulp down a bitter tonic of UPS job pocket the
tarnished college dreams: **it's hard to dream**. that shore's an empty cup with
nothin to fill you up so take one last look and

run

dive

into cloudy nights in a beer bottle smoky moons in a swisher flying fields
of green stars that blink like traffic lights concrete freeways that dip
and glide press rusty fingers into radio station buttons that glow
like seashells on stick charts ride the steel hull of minivans and
suv's coast along coconut hair to hips lips that praise reggae suns
praise gods on basketball courts in softball dugouts have mercy
for aloha shirt muscles bristling beneath the earth of your skin
you warriors who war and celebrate weekend breaks and when
this daylight brakes this is when you
break.

CRASH

By the side of a looming mountain my friend and I
staggered away
tiny and scared
from a silver beast
flipped over and smashed
to glass pieces
cold mortality dripping down my forehead
sliced skin flapping against my palm

flannel draped white samaritans blew smoke in my eyes
threw camouflage hunting jackets on me
hollered *WE*
pointing to themselves
calling 9-1-1! YOU
pointing to me
bloody!
Cold? Shiver shiver?
How many fingers?
Dos?
Traayaz?

Strapped
into a rolling ambulance
a sugar blond nurse
asked me how to spell my name
seven times
giggled. every time
eyed me with suspicion
Are you Indian?

In the hospital a male nurse
strung stitches
through the blooming wounds in my wrists
the only remains
of the passenger window
His blue aloha shirt

reminded me of home
I wanted to tell him I wasn't from here
I wanted to tell him I missed my mom
I wanted to tell him I was scared
of dying in someone else's country

As whimpers escaped from my lips
he yanked the black thread just
a little
tighter
sealing my voice into my wrists

At my friend's house
I leaned against a porcelain shower stall
yearned
to be diluted
into waters
clear of color

when I turned the knob of the shower off
I suddenly remembered
her entirely corn blond family

Desperate
I searched the bathroom
swept
wiped
scooped
gathered
my swirls of long curly black hair
wary
of leaving any
trace

LAST DAYS IN THE BAY

my last days as a bay area kid was high top sneakers **sliding** off my feet and into your bed white sage burning black your eyes **sliding** down my lips shattuck concrete grips our hips as we slither like the **sliding** lizard on your wooden box we bart into frisco fog i watch a soggy sun **sliding** down the blue glow of my cell phone i catch tears on your swisher **sliding** dry as ghost town sundays together we shoplift sliced mango moments **sliding** into reggae nights i wind this clock never want to stop time is running **out**.

TELL THEM

SPOKEN MARSHALLESE LESSON NINE

You will often be questioned by other Marshallese, especially those born and raised at home. This is a good chance to practice the proper response (you will practice as B).

A: Kwōjeḷā ke eọñwōd? Do you know how to fish?
B: Ijaje. Kwōmaroñ ke katakin eō? I don't know how. Can you teach me?

A: Kwōjeḷā ke inọñ? Do you know how to tell Marshallese legends/stories?
B: Ijaje. Kwōmaroñ ke katakin eō? I don't know how. Can you teach me?

A: Kwōjeḷā ke kowainini? Do you know how to pick coconuts?
B: Ijaje. Kwōmaroñ ke katakin eō? I don't know how. Can you teach me?

A: Kwōjeḷā ke uṃuṃ ma? Do you know how to cook breadfruit in the earth?
B. Ijaje. Kwōmaroñ ke katakin eō? I don't know how. Can you teach me?

A: Ijjab kanooj jeḷā, ak inaaj kajjioñ. I'm not an expert—but I can try.

JUST A ROCK

My mother says

Go—look. It's Lidepdepju

    the legend, the goddess, the beautiful.

But all I see

is a rock

on the reef.

CAMPAIGNING IN AUR

I.

After six hours on a ship, women
spill from the fiberglass mouth
of bubbling speedboats, women
in popsicle colored baseball caps and silk
guams, faded muumuus, and flowered
pohnpeian skirts, whooping, hollering, laughing
in the Aur water.

My mother is running for the Aur Atoll senator's seat.
Throughout all the elections, 32 senators elected
were men.
Throughout all the elections, only 1 senator elected
was a woman.

My mother knows the stakes
She knows the odds are slim
So she disembarks on her motherisland flanked
by a campaign army
of women.

For a few of them
this is their first time back home
after so many years.
For me and my cousin
this is our first time ever.

II.

My mother informs us—
the youngest of the crew—
that this is no vacation cruise no
jambo we're here to work.
So we unroll the bags, help string up lights
wake up at dawn and trudge door to door
filming, snapping photographs, both of us
hauling stacks of fliers listing
my mother's genealogy
her work history
and her campaign promises.

We march
beneath the shade of gnarled breadfruit trees thicker
than any I've ever seen, dodge
barking dogs with bared
teeth, pass concrete shells
of abandoned houses and curious children
threading through grass as tall as our knees.

As we march she stops to talk
to a man who husks white flakes
into a plastic orange basin, surrounded
by an audience of bloated bags of coconuts.
She talks to the woman who stitches spiderwebs
of pandanus leaves from rolls and rolls
of sun-dried plaits stacked around her.

At night we help the other women fill plastic plates
meant to persuade
the bellies of ri-Aur
seated,
at the feet
of my mother,
her voice
amplified.

III.

This is my mother promising a change
This is my aunty stirring a large pot of homemade stew
This is my cousin promoting WUTMI—a nonprofit for women
This is another aunty discussing healthy eating
This is another aunty stringing flower leis
This is a cousin strumming an ukulele and singing
This is a grandma telling us stories
of what Aur used to be
This is the mother of all mothers
standing in the oceanside
watching

IV.

And this is my cousin and I
running away
into tangled leaves
climbing moss
and whispering bushes
where we splash into water
clear as a mirror, the sky—
a giant empty canvas
We emerge, hair still wet
as we stroll beneath
a warm rain that drizzles on our face
Aunties we've just met
call us into their smoky
cook houses where fresh tonaj, hot
and soft melt in our mouths

And as we fall asleep on a sun worn jaki
we fall asleep as girls
listening to the women the women the women
talkingwhisperinglaughing
we fall asleep and dream
the women we hope to one day be.

TELL THEM

I prepared the package
for my friends in the states
First—the dangling earrings, woven
into half-moons black pearls glinting
like an eye in a storm of tight spirals

Second—the baskets
sturdy, also woven
brown cowry shells shiny
intricate mandalas shaped
by calloused fingers

Inside I write a message:

Wear these earrings
to parties classes and meetings
to the corner store the grocery store
and while riding the bus

Store jewelry, incense, copper coins
and curling letters like this one
in this basket

And when others ask you
where you got this
you tell them

       They're from the Marshall Islands

Show them where it is on a map
Tell them we are a proud people
toasted dark brown as the carved ribs
of a tree stump

Tell them we are descendants
of the finest navigators
in the world

Tell them our islands were dropped
from a basket
carried by a giant

Tell them we are the hollow hulls
of canoes as fast as the wind
slicing through the pacific sea

We are wood shavings
and drying pandanus leaves
and sticky bwiros at kemems

Tell them we are sweet harmonies
of grandmothers mothers aunties sisters—
songs late into night

Tell them we are whispered prayers
the breath of God
a crown of fuchsia flowers encircling
Aunty Mary's white sea foam hair

Tell them we are styrofoam cups of koolaid red
waiting patiently for the ilomij

We are papaya golden sunsets bleeding
into a glittering open sea
We are skies uncluttered
majestic in their sweeping landscape
We are the ocean
terrifying and regal in its power

Tell them we are dusty rubber slippers swiped
from concrete doorsteps
We are the ripped seams and the broken
door handles of taxis

We are sweaty hands shaking
another sweaty hand in heat
Tell them we are days and nights hotter
than anything you can imagine

We are little girls with braids
cartwheeling beneath the rain

We are shards of broken beer bottles
burrowed beneath fine white sand
We are children flinging
like rubber bands
across a road clogged with chugging cars
Tell them
we only have one road

And after all this
tell them about the water—how we have seen it rising
flooding across our cemeteries
gushing over the sea walls
and crashing against our homes

Tell them what it's like
to see the entire ocean__level___with the land

Tell them
we are afraid .

Tell them we don't know
of the politics
or the science
but tell them we see
what is in our own backyard

Tell them that some of us
are old fishermen who believe that God
made us a promise
Tell them some of us
are a little bit more skeptical

But most importantly you tell them
we don't want to leave
we've never wanted to leave

and that we

are nothing

without our islands

LAVENDER SALTWATER

dedicated to our doula, Grace Alvaro Caligtan

Waves of
contractions
crash
into me
crack me
open split
down the middle

I imagine
the eruption: a bulging
sack of slime and blood and
spit

Do not measure
the breaths the minutes
the hours of clenched
fists curled toes
eyes pinched
shut tight
closed

Just inhale
the saving
Grace
of hot towels dipped
in sweet lavender

Dream of saltwater
orange fruit and sunsets
Uncle Clyde Aunty Kaka
Mom Hetine Tamera
Baby Dukie all of us
that one picnic afternoon
that ordinary sunday

just think
of her
seeing it all
someday

And when she
is pulled
from my body
an army of white
coats shout
an order:

OPEN
YOUR
EYES

And there she is.

DEAR MATAFELE PEINAM

Dear Matafele Peinam,

You are a seven month old sunrise of gummy smiles
you are bald as an egg and bald as the buddha
you are thighs that are thunder
shrieks that are lightning
so excited for bananas, hugs and
our morning walks past the lagoon

Dear Matafele Peinam,

I want to tell you about that lagoon
that lucid, sleepy lagoon
lounging against the sunrise

Men say that one day
that lagoon will devour you

They say it will gnaw at the shoreline
chew at the roots of your breadfruit trees
gulp down rows of your seawalls
and crunch your island's shattered bones

They say you, your daughter
and your granddaughter, too
will wander
rootless
with only
a passport
to call home

*Originally performed at the 2014 Opening Ceremony of the United Nations Secretary-General's Climate Summit.

Dear Matafele Peinam,

Don't cry
Mommy promises you

no one
will come and devour you

no greedy whale of a company sharking through political seas
no backwater bullying of businesses with broken morals
no blindfolded bureaucracies gonna push
this mother ocean over
the edge

no one's drowning, baby

no one's moving
no one's losing
their homeland
no one's gonna become
a climate change refugee

or should i say
no one else

to the Carteret Islanders of Papua New Guinea
and to the Taro Islanders of the Solomon Islands
I take this moment
to apologize to you
we are drawing the line
here

Because baby we are going to fight
your mommy daddy
bubu jimma your country and your president too
we will all fight

and even though there are those
hidden behind platinum titles

who like to pretend
that we don't exist
that the Marshall Islands
Tuvalu
Kiribati
Maldives
Typhoon Haiyan in the Philippines
floods of Pakistan, Algeria, Colombia
and all the hurricanes, earthquakes, and tidalwaves
didn't exist

still
there are those
who see us

hands reaching out
fists raising up
banners unfurling
megaphones booming
and we are

canoes blocking coal ships

the radiance of solar villages

the rich clean soil of the farmer's past

petitions blooming from teenage fingertips

families biking, recycling, reusing,
engineers dreaming, designing, building,
artists painting, dancing, writing,
and we are spreading the word

and there are thousands
out on the street
marching with signs
hand in hand
chanting for change NOW

and they're marching for you, baby
they're marching for us

because we deserve
to do more
than just
survive
we deserve
to thrive

Dear Matafele Peinam,

you are eyes heavy
with drowsy weight
so just close those eyes, baby
and sleep in peace

because we won't let you down

you'll see

THERE'S A JOURNALIST HERE

There's a journalist here
who wants to interview you

they want to hear
about your house
older than you
its cracked plywood walls
like dry, sunburnt skin
how it collapsed
like a lung
as the water rushed in
they want to hear
about your journal
how you woke
to soggy pages—ink
staining the floor
staining your hands
they want to hear
about the glass shards
from your window
how they carved
jagged pathways
along your stepmother's leg

they want to hear
how you blame yourself
the way the neighbors
blamed you

> women
> shouldn't stare
> at the ocean
> too long

> it was your
> boldness
> that dared it to come

that's
what they want to hear

they don't want to hear
that maybe
you're imagining

a new house
with doors
clear windows
on a grassy hillside
they don't want to hear that
weeks later
you found your breath
filling and expanding your lungs
that all you want now
is to move

forward

TWO DEGREES

The other night my 1-year-old was a fever
pressed against my chest

We wrestled with a thermometer
that read
99.8 degrees
the doctor says
technically
100.4
is a fever
but I can see her flushed face
how she drapes
across my lap, listless

LiPeinam is usually a
wobbly walking
toddler all chunks and
duck-footed shaky knees
stomping squeaky yellow
light up shoes across
the edge of the reef

And I think
what a difference
a few degrees
can make

Scientists say
if humans warm the world
more than 2 degrees
then catastrophe will hit
Imagine North American wildfires increasing by 400 percent
animal extinction rising by 30 percent
fresh water declining by 20 percent
thousands, millions displaced
left wandering

wondering
what
happened?

At a climate change conference
a colleague tells me 2 degrees
is just a benchmark for negotiations
I tell him for my islands 2 degrees
is a gamble
at 2 degrees my islands
will already be under water
this is why our leaders push
for **1.5**

Seems small
like **0.5** degrees
shouldn't matter
like **0.5** degrees
are just crumbs
like the Marshall Islands
must look
on a map
just crumbs you
dust off the table, wipe
your hands clean of

Today LiPeinam is feeling better
she bobs around our backyard
drops pebbles and leaves
into a plastic bucket
before emptying the bucket out
and dropping pebbles in again

As I watch I think about futility
I think about the world
making the same mistakes
since the industrial revolution
since 1977
when a scientist said 2 degrees
was the estimate

On Kili island
the tides were underestimated
patients sleeping in a clinic with
a nuclear history threaded
into their bloodlines woke
to a wild water world
a rushing rapid of salt
a sewage of syringes and gauze

Later
they wheeled their hospital beds out
let them rest in the sun
they must be
stained rusted our people
creaking brackish from
salt spray and radiation blasts
so so tired, wandering wondering
if the world will
wheel us out to rest in the sun
will they just dust
their hands of us, wipe
them clean

My father told me that idik
—when the tide is nearest an equilibrium
is the best time for fishing

Maybe I'm
writing the tide towards
an equilibrium
willing the world
to find its balance

So that people
remember
that beyond
the discussions
numbers
and statistics

there are faces
all the way out here
there is
a toddler
stomping squeaky
yellow light up shoes
across the edge of a reef

not yet
under water

BASKET

woman
tip your lid
across the land
you swell

with

offering

you

offer

offer

offer

a seabed
to scrape
a receptacle
to dump
with scraps

your
body
is a country
we conquer
and devour

we
take
and
we
take

and
you
keep
giving

woman
tip your lid
across the land
you swell
           with
              offering
                  you
                      offer
                          offer
                            offer

                                    a lineage
                                  of sand

                                      a reef
                                      of memory

                                        your womb
                                      the sustainer

                                    of life

                                  I fell asleep

                              dreamt

                        my words

                    were

                a current

           flowing
    to greet you

ABOUT THE AUTHOR

Kathy Jetñil-Kijiner is a poet of Marshallese ancestry who was born in the Marshall Islands and raised in Hawai'i. Bearing witness at the front lines of various activist movements inspires her work and has propelled her poetry to audiences ranging from elementary school students to more than a hundred world leaders at the United Nations Climate Summit in 2014, where she performed a poem to her daughter, "Dear Matafele Peinam." She has been featured by CNN, Democracy Now, Mother Jones, the *Huffington Post*, NBC News, *National Geographic*, *Vogue Magazine*, Nobel Women's Initiative, and more. Currently, Jetñil-Kijiner teaches Pacific studies courses at the College of the Marshall Islands. She also helped establish and is now co-director of the Mashall Islands–based nonprofit Jo-Jikum, which empowers Marshallese youth to develop solutions to environmental issues threatening their home islands.